It Shouldn't Have Been Beautiful

It Shouldn't Have Been

Beautiful

Lia Purpura

PENGUIN POETS

PENGUIN BOOKS
An imprint of Penguin Random House LLC
375 Hudson Street
New York, New York 10014
penguin.com

LIBRARY OF CONGRESS CATALOGING-IN-PUBLICATION DATA

Purpura, Lia.
[Poems. Selections]
It shouldn't have been beautiful / Lia Purpura.
pages ; cm. — (Penguin Poets)
ISBN 978-0-14-312690-4 (paperback)
I. Title.   II. Title: It should not have been beautiful.
PS3566.U67A6 2015
811'.54—dc23
2015016943

Printed in the United States of America
1   3   5   7   9   10   8   6   4   2

Set in ITC Garamond Book Std
Designed by Ginger Legato

For Jed and Joseph

CONTENTS

ACKNOWLEDGMENTS

Grateful acknowledgment is made to the following publications, in whose pages these poems first appeared:

Antioch Review, "Proximities" and "Time"

The Georgia Review, "Gratitude," "Accident," and "Belief"

Make Magazine, "Universal Principle"

The New Republic, "Net"

The New Yorker, "Allegories," "Prayer" (p. 8), "First Leaf," "Beginning," "Future Perfect," "Probability," and "Study with Melon"

Orion Magazine, "Design"

Plume, "Rare Moment," "Loud Walk in Fall," "Regret," and "Wall Calendar"

The Southern Review, "Proof"

Third Coast, "Red Bird in Snow"

My thanks to Matt McGowan, Ann Pancake, and Paul Slovak, all of whom, in their way, have seen these poems into being. And to Jed Gaylin, first reader, true north.

It Shouldn't Have Been Beautiful

I

Belief

Light being
wavy and particulate
at once
is instructive –
why wouldn't
other things or states
present as
both/and?
For instance
I both
believe and can't.
Holding these
together produces
a wobble, I think
it's time
to take seriously
as a stance.

First Leaf

That yellow
was a falling-off,
a fall
for once I saw
coming –
it could
in its stillness
still be turned from,
it was not
yet ferocious,
its hold drew me,
was a shiny switch plate
in the otherwise dark,
rash, ongoing green,
a green so hungry
for light and air that
part gave up,
went alone,
chose to leave,
and by choosing
embellishment
got seen.

Design

Here is the day, sun, gulls
backlit and cresting,
a jackhammer
suggesting I'm
here but not really
in it, I'm more
representative
of a person in early
ambient fall,
near a fountain, and Thursday
farmers' market –
like an architect's model,
precise, small me,
stuck on a bench
reading a book, lending an air
of things going too fast.

Uncertainty

It's not a place,
but I am grateful to be in it,
where endings and known things
complicate,
and I, the judge I know myself to be,
go to review
the very heavy declarations
I so often lay down like law.
It's not a place at all.
I just practice there, assemble
some beliefs, disturb
others and put the extras
into a pile for mosaics,
one of my big projects
for the future.

Forensic

One aggrieved person
acting alone or
the force of a movement –
how should we see it?
Return to a moment
and set up a scene,
offer contingencies,
freeze some frames.
It was/it wasn't
intentional.
So few are trained
to read events
from beginning to end.
How clear and bright and cold
the dots are.
Still, we have to be
so far away
before they constellate.

Prayer

Its occasion
could be
a spot of sun,
bar sign, label
on jeans,
carnation, red
light where you
wait and
gratitude hits.
Or a name
the length
of a subway car
that only makes sense
when you say it aloud
in your head
as it passes.

Determinism

"Storm Targets Midwest" –
as if after deep consideration
or in a passionate fit,
the sky chose
them and not us.
That's one way to ride
the day's events
into meaning.

Red Leaf

It's precious
little warmth
the trees are giving,
muddled with last greens,
addled with vines
and that red,
a new cry
at dusk –
oh mind
where all things
freshly darkened
meet.

Regret

It's definitely a place.
A land
I wish I hadn't
visited, but
I belong there.
It's a field,
it's wide
and operates
by admitting
new thoughts,
by charging
admission.
It was expensive there
once, very costly,
but not
until now.

Doomsday/Rapture

The world will end again
soon.
From now on
it's late.
Plan for the day:
divest and spend
everything,
apologize, neaten,
hope not to rise
unto a morning
stuck in its course
exploding in sunlight
as usual.

Lifting

Things face off –
and not that one
wins, but
tensions shift,
surges work
resistant levers,
and passing
from state to state
unlodges
forces in the body
that wake,
oppose,
then
lighten loads.

Story

Every morning
four or five
small birds chase a hawk
from a stand of pines –
another drama
in my west-facing window
like sunset, dependable,
but fast with sharp turns,
diving and sparring,
one party or the other
not getting the point
so it has to keep happening:
one's an intruder,
hungry, insistent, there's
threat and defense,
there's persistence, desire
I greet, expect now,
welcome in.

Loud Walk in Fall

There is something else
noise hurts.
Not just me.
Flinching abounds
in the open air
which hasn't a body,
but still, is bare
and has been
walked in on.
That truck with no muffler
embarrassed it.

Sadness, Restaurant

A certain kind
comes very fast,
but unexpectedly,
like a feeling about
work on behalf
of beauty
no one
devours:
those carrot birds,
those radish flowers.

Weed

Its precondition
is uselessness –
wrong in its place,
bobbing in wind,
fattening in sun, red
seeds in a cloak
with an orange ruff
whatever that is,
Bittersweet, maybe.

Some Beauty

Its nature
is ruthless, nothing
as simple as
loss being ruinous,
those undeniable rainbows
of oil, shock of bright
sulphurous puddles
(in goldfinch, in lemon)
and now what,
if that beauty's
terrible plumage
makes you keep looking
and disturbs your despair.

Field, Late Fall

Where the light's from
isn't clear, but
illumination as
bestowed
insists.
I'm more inclined
to think
from within
(each blade
of grass
its own fire,
the whole field
blazing up
like a rough lake,
or scrap pile).
Without or within,
pain, too, is good
at blurring
its origins.

Fluency

To sew the blue-burnt
edges of a gunshot wound
together
should require only
concentration,
training, deftness,
ease with systems
awry and how to
stabilize, but
with good tools,
sharp blades,
bright lights,
I'm guessing
a material's
qualities become
more.
Professionals
are adept
at covering it up, but
I'm pretty sure
pleasure insists.

Study with Melon

The stem end of a melon
is web-like, form
finding a pattern
that's thinking itself
a density
a concentration
beginning a line
then casting it out
and moving on from,
an order established,
a gesture complete.
Completion: how
someone at a distance
might see it.

II

Beginning

In the beginning,
in the list of begats,
one begat
got forgot:
work begets work
(one poem
bears
the next).
In other words,
once there was air,
a bird
could be got.
Not taken.
Not kept.
But conjured up.

Hope

To feel the slightest
breeze come on
but not expect it
to last, though
it *is* a lifting,
relief
that's been scarce –
you can't help
noting
the drop in degrees,
but it might not
be a real change
in weather,
you might overheat it,
or scare it
by speaking its name, so
hold back, learn to say
not just yet,
I won't rush it
and no, I'm not dying
for a very small sip of
whatever that was
in the trees.

Lost Day

The hours aren't latching on
or hooking in. At all.
There isn't any nap
to catch.
They're sliding around
in disguise
like gods. It's two
in the afternoon. It's four.
You can't take these hours
apart and repair them.
Nothing's wrong
with them.
They aren't broken.

Distance

It can be
overridden,
or bridged
and ridden into,
golden and shining,
promising, but
it's better dimmed
which lets you be
in the in-between
states, hours, etc.
and not so
irritable and squinty.

Natural Disaster

That someone has less
might make you
happy with yours –
or unhappy
to think about
portions at all.
Those who have
very little,
studies say, are more
inclined to
give half away.
Maybe being closer
to nothing
makes stuff
not matter so much,
(or a few things
matter a lot).
Maybe gratitude
isn't best measured
by comparison.

Ice Shelf (Larsen B)

It's not the kind of seep
that puddles
but over time
(it should've been
millennia)
forces cracks so
even a tiny thaw at the edge
indicates a problem
not an abstraction –
that is, if it all melts
seas will rise 190 feet.
Another fact is
sun diamonds up fields
of dew in the morning,
brightens cuffs of barbed wire,
transluces new leaves.
Beauty persists.
Which, as truths go,
complicates
all we need to know.

History

Burned to the ground
means nothing's left
but the need to say it,
very intense, the flames
kicked up by
terrible winds
took the house and
nothing was left,
a few tools
in the billets, nothing
worth keeping but
burned to the ground,
which accompanies
disbelief,
makes a scene
with woods out back,
fills the space where
once a house stood
with something,
a story at least
to pass on to the kids.

Rare Moment

A clear choice
is so sweet. Not
reluctance but
real resistance.
Joy-to-bursting,
or none.
Grief,
not gradations.
Someone essential
and someone not.
A good, dark
strike-through
versus
weighing everything
at the end of each day.
Look, a cat killed a cardinal
on an emerald lawn.
For so many reasons
it shouldn't have been
beautiful.
But that's also
the kind of book
I like best.

Net

I want to go back
to the way I lived before
when, turning, I'd be
up against
a wall of books
not a room for chats,
wanteds, want-yous,
for-sale lists, lists
of meetings in space,
which is nowhere –
a time when I had
a pine floor to wander
and boredom was good,
a cool drink
I took in so
I could return to work
refreshed, no hope,
just secret
negotiations with hope
taking place.

Relativity

Shade can chill
or relieve
and sun
comfort or oppress,
depending on
what you need
to shed or retain,
which is nothing
as simple as
sin being dark,
and grace, light.
Filaments in a web
can be both invisible
and bright.
Each thing's
its own partner,
each always both,
depending on
where you stand,
not so central, not so
always commanding.

Crape Myrtle

There's the crape myrtle
that shattered me
or I shattered it
or we both
in its silence or
mine stood
and rooted and unrooted
time, in the morning
between us was nothing
but moments, magenta,
majestic, commanding
something,
I don't know
what it meant, it kept
meaning
roughly, but
maybe that's me
making it
more, or ferocious,
wider,
wanting the tree
to come even closer.

Tropism

Plants are very slow.
You have to slow way down
to observe a plant's decisions,
(networks, rhizomatics
that look so like our
will, intention),
then there's the question
of consciousness
(no central brain,
though adaptations like
go *around* the rock,
share, unify,
tide others over
during dry spells)
or what else to call it
(intelligence, thinking?)
this way of being
not paralyzed
by the problem at hand.

Prayer

Some roteness,
words in certain
orders, bent knees,
a more
confined space
to occupy –
a more formal
attitude might work,
the way
a smaller suitcase
makes packing
less puzzling.

Proximities

A man walks into a coffee shop.
But it's not a joke.
I bought coffee there
last summer.
Small, with milk.
It's never a joke
to walk in or out of a shop
unharmed. It's easy
to forget
you aren't a person
being shot at.
I'm not.
I wasn't, though
I was there
last summer.
Not-shot-at
and I never knew it.
Did not once
think it.
Thinking it now
the moment thins,
it sheers
and I move back
to other coffee shops
where I never fell, or bled,
and then
I sit for a while
with my regular cup
and feel things collapse
or go on, I can't tell.

Wall Calendar

That's one day
fewer
you get to have.
One you had
and lived
that's gone.
Crossed out.
You get more,
but dosed
and measured
(though with
one line
you can make
a day into
two triangles,
a week of sailboats,
a month
of good, hard,
sideways rain).

Proof

That goldfinches favor
yellow blooms
is proof
that sustenance
comes in a form
resembling, pleasing,
not to be fought for
but found
like bearings
by a light both
given and sought,
that singular glow.

Talisman

The act
of granting powers
to a rock
so it can be used
to conjure luck,
it worked before
it might again,
how small
and irregular
this matter of
millions of years
of compression
and icebergs melting
ending here,
deep in a pocket,
at work
on the course
of a diagnosis.

City

Everyone's someone
or just looks like them
in the shoulders,
countenance, bearing,
is famous or once was
and look, buying milk,
the paper, a danish,
those keys in her pocket
warming, poking
someone like me,
who might be
someone, who
has my eyes.

Plaques

Plaques everywhere
studding the day
would make beholding
easier.
And everything a scenic view:
Here a wick
of forsythia shot up.
Here a shadow-as-steed
rode the lawn
right out of its
useless, modern
detachment.

III

Make It New

In rejecting things
that stand in for
(robins: spring),
why be so strict?
Why resist
the usual likenesses?
Because hope
needs inventing,
its forms need adapting.
Toss the old ones
into the pile
so we, our unlikely
small neighborhood,
might win
the city-wide
recycling competition.
Spring startles,
weighs nothing,
and is endlessly
free.

Desire

It's not enough,
but it is, because
too much
would topple
all I could hold.
More wouldn't be
enough either,
it would
wear out in time
and then nothing
would be enough.
It just
wouldn't.

Accident

There was a train so perfectly wrecked,
let's see, the paper says
jackknifed. But that isn't right.
A jackknife's only briefly bent
before it snaps into place.
Cleanly snaps.
Like a thought you saw coming.
Not one you didn't.

Shell

What comes off
in bits or
more whole
and in curves
gets piled neatly
or scattered
or crushed
depending on
hunger, urgency,
or attitudes
about fragility.

Impurities

All the salt glaze
mottlings,
rough patches, whorls,
nicks you didn't expect,
those degradations
and transformations –
some poisons
are very sweet.
A glassy black
branch of coal
is chic now
in a vase
and filters from air
who knows what.
Stuff we shouldn't be
breathing.
Lacy, sheer,
floating things
that if magnified
you'd want to keep.

Devices

Time was different –
if it was dead
we filled it
with thoughts, trees
along the interstate
we occupied
by seeing,
and power lines
rising and dipping,
we wore those
by trying on a phrase
they necklaced by.
There weren't
so many ways
to counter the distance
everywhere.
It was just fine being
human and lonely.

Virtual

So many things are enhanced,
so many ways of being
are calculated on
your behalf
to provide
an experience.
Between body and world,
blue screens and encryptions
work hard to help you
seem to be here.

Creation

I want to get
a feeling
right,
not sensation,
clip art, cut
and spliced
brief samplings
of Michelangelo,
but exactly the whitish-blue
space between
God's finger and Adam's,
the not-yet
created
in that gap,
the moment held,
so the world becoming
cannot be made
to refer to
anything else.

Light

In watching
it pass
you can't see it
passing,
slipped into
day, or
absorbed into
night,
it's both
slow
and over with
at the same time.

Line

Drawing one's
useful, the need
is clear.
It's not a real
threshold,
just an idea,
or else
nothing means.
There are lines to stay
behind: ropes
with latches
officials undo
to let some pass.
The dip in the center
suggests
you could step right over
but either
haven't yet or won't.

Early Spring

Everywhere is
something to do,
take up, or take care of.
Nothing
makes me more
useful – it's more
useful than anything
to stop,
to watch spring,
to interrupt spring
and feel with two fingers
along my jawbone –
how I'd be
without skin,
pursue that.

Object/Desire

I think I don't want it.
But then, it's right there.
I could turn and just grab it,
though having would end
the now-brightened moment,
so adequate unto itself.
I could help things along,
look out the window
at the green wall of
tree upon tree,
and make that suffice,
the distance please,
which isn't the same
as the thing
I want, then don't want,
dear moment I so much don't want
to erase.

Upgrade

It feels wrong
to have,
it's so
easy to use –
the old wasn't
bad, just
that's all there was.
Now there's more.
And what I had
for so long,
all that
time while waiting
for things to kick on,
to warm up
is gone.

Start Again

This starling-streaked air
is a door
(more people
lose trains of thought
at thresholds
than anywhere else)
which if you step through
means shedding, leaving
(can't say what for what),
admitting it's messy
each spring to be
wind-blown and shattered
like petals, like eggshells.

Drive

The light
this morning's
so sharp –
was it then?
Is a hook
how time
bends?
Then
was a drive
in vast country
with Bighorns,
and this
is a fenced
lot of trees
and morning
sidling, over-
laying, a graft
taking, then
it's a blade
stripping away
so one sees
right into the core
time leaves.

Redemptive Arc

Maybe more
a line
cast out
that floats
on rough water,
not a frayed
and chicken-pecked
lasso, which is
how a story
feels when it
tries too hard.
Best would be
the hovering trail
of the bouncing ball
that accompanied
old cartoon songs,
whose moves
and pauses,
precise, inflected,
helped everyone
follow along.

Universal Principle

It begins
with nothing
and then becomes
a knot.
Things shift.
Soon
everything has
a mind,
and nothing
is waiting
to see if
we'll notice.

Time

Having only a little means
you take
what you've got
or, because
it's not worth enough, you
don't – like not picking up
a penny because
it's only a little luck.

Probability

Most coincidences are not
miraculous, but way more
common than we think –
it's the shiver
of noticing being
central in a sequence
of events
that makes so much
seem wild and rare –
because what if it wasn't?
Astonishment's nothing
without your consent.

IV

Allegories

That crag, in its hunching,
suggests a shawl
under which we can slip
our burdens, since
we alone among creatures
bestow likenesses
for assurance
we really exist,
and name boulders and peaks
Widow's this, Widow's that,
so others might navigate
by the forms
of our grief.

Old World

Teach that its objects
have dispositions
(visages, comports)
and belong to a time
(an era, an epoch)
so it's clear
how things worked:
people sat down
and made things
to last, for you
who were real
to them even
before you were born.

Winter Night

It nibbles
on the horizon,
then
its quiet
magnifies space,
then us,
until we break
into so many pieces
to which it responds
with indifference
we say –
though really
that's just
an enormity
of the cold
and dark
variety.

You

The chance of it being
you who are born
or meeting
anyone who comes to be
friend, beloved,
all the improbables
flying around,
lining up
day after day –
how does that come to
look like a week
then years,
and the waking
each morning
expected.

Birthright

As if
under every
nutshell
were something.
And what kind
of game
is that,
with no chance
for nothing
in the end.

Perspective

It's exactly
when I point and say
see that blue boat –
that I'm no longer sure
what I'm pointing to,
and a gap opens fast
into which falls
all I expected
you to say.

Forces

An invisible field,
if hit, makes
real particles exist,
changing entirely
what nothing
means,
and also the weight
of emptiness.

Gratitude

It softens want
into nothing mean
and lack is not
so dark anymore.
Things can be
a little dim,
less than ideal
and still amaze,
as when there's been
enough grief
and you aren't any longer
bowing to it.
One day,
the pain having stopped,
isn't a moment.
It isn't brief.
It keeps going.

Chosen

It could've been
an everyday
brown-and-cream
sparrow, or grackle
with oily rainbow wings
but so near my eye,
its robe, its sash,
its fire, flare, gash –
it's visiting me.
Hard to think
otherwise.

Solitude

No one home.
Snow packing
the morning in.
Much white
nothing filling up.
A V of birds
pulling
the silence
until some dog
across the street
barks, and breaks
what I call my peace.
What a luxury
annoyance is.
It bites off
and keeps
just enough of
what I think
I want to be endless.

Lines

I count on
lines drawn,
the air
of not saying
too much,
even the unsaid-
as-glance
helps things
not go
too far, too fast.
The cost
of overabundance
is steep.
Lines
make you mind
what you want to keep.

Red Bird in Snow

You can choose
to stop short –
or have it
not matter,
not weigh
the brightness,
not hold
very still
and be
known
to yourself
again.
A thing
fills
with exactly
the radiance
you accord it.

Insufficiency

Now
feels lessened
because I couldn't
muster my best
then.
(What a long
reflection
then casts.)
Or fix things.
Oh, my love's
good
but undercut
by all I couldn't
make better –
no matter
I wasn't
born yet.

Ditch

A curb works by
running right up
alongside –
so when you
curb something,
hold it back,
rein it in,
it won't become
an overgrown
and deepened
darkness
you have to get
yourself
winched out of.

Lit

If you're *lit*
you mean to say
against gray,
pallor, darkness.
Against sun
would mean
nothing, you'd be
wholly absorbed,
so when you say *lit*
you're implying
something.
You might not
intend to
but no one *lit*
(from within, or up)
says so
without meaning
what's all around
isn't.

Sunday

Signs come.
For what
I don't know.
To be one
in a vastness
without meaning,
except for
making something of it,
except for it being
a conversation
I'm not holding
alone.

Gone

It's that, when I'm gone
(and right off this is tricky),
I won't be worried
about being gone.
I won't be here
to miss anything.
I want now, sure,
all I've been gathering
since I was born,
but later,
when I no longer have it,
being gone (perhaps
a state everlasting,
who knows),
this moment
(stand closer, love,
you can't be too close),
is not a thing I'll know to miss.
I doubt I'll miss it.
I can't get over this.

Future Perfect

Where you were
before you were born,
and where you are
when you're not anymore
might be very close.
Might be the same place,
though neither is
as slippery
as being here but
imagining where
you will have been –
that point
where things land,
are finished, over, and
gone but not yet.

Photo by Alan Kolc

Lia Purpura is the author of seven collections of essays, poems, and translations, most recently *Rough Likeness* (essays) and *King Baby* (poems). She was a National Book Critics Circle Award finalist (for *On Looking*), and her other honors include a Guggenheim Foundation fellowship, National Endowment for the Arts and Fulbright fellowships, three Pushcart Prizes, the Associated Writing Programs Award in Nonfiction, and the Beatrice Hawley and Ohio State University Press awards in poetry. Recent work appears in *Agni, Field, The Georgia Review, Orion, The New Republic, The New Yorker, The Paris Review, Best American Essays*, and elsewhere. She is Writer in Residence at the University of Maryland, Baltimore County, and a member of the core faculty at the Rainier Writing Workshop. Lia Purpura lives in Baltimore, Maryland.

JOHN ASHBERY
Selected Poems
Self-Portrait in a Convex Mirror

TED BERRIGAN
The Sonnets

LAUREN BERRY
The Lifting Dress

JOE BONOMO
Installations

PHILIP BOOTH
Lifelines: Selected Poems,
*   1950–1999*
Selves

JULIANNE BUCHSBAUM
The Apothecary's Heir

JIM CARROLL
Fear of Dreaming:
*   The Selected Poems*
Living at the Movies
Void of Course

ALISON HAWTHORNE DEMING
Genius Loci
Rope

CARL DENNIS
Another Reason
Callings
New and Selected Poems
*   1974–2004*
Practical Gods
Ranking the Wishes
Unknown Friends

DIANE DI PRIMA
Loba

STUART DISCHELL
Backwards Days
Dig Safe

STEPHEN DOBYNS
Velocities: New and Selected
*   Poems, 1966–1992*

EDWARD DORN
Way More West: New and
*   Selected Poems*

ROGER FANNING
The Middle Ages

ADAM FOULDS
The Broken Word

CARRIE FOUNTAIN
Burn Lake
Instant Winner

AMY GERSTLER
Crown of Weeds:
*   Poems*
Dearest Creature
Ghost Girl
Medicine
Nerve Storm
Scattered at Sea

EUGENE GLORIA
Drivers at the Short-Time
*   Motel*
Hoodlum Birds
My Favorite Warlord

DEBORA GREGER
By Herself
Desert Fathers, Uranium
*   Daughters*
God
Men, Women, and Ghosts
Western Art

TERRANCE HAYES
Hip Logic
How to be Drawn
Lighthead
Wind in a Box

NATHAN HOKS
The Narrow Circle

ROBERT HUNTER
Sentinel and Other Poems

MARY KARR
Viper Rum

WILLIAM KECKLER
Sanskrit of the Body

JACK KEROUAC
Book of Sketches
Book of Blues
Book of Haikus

JOANNA KLINK
Circadian
Excerpts from a Secret
*   Prophecy*
Raptus

JOANNE KYGER
As Ever:
*   Selected Poems*

ANN LAUTERBACH
Hum
If in Time: Selected Poems,
*   1975–2000*
On a Stair
Or to Begin Again
Under the Sign

CORINNE LEE
PYX

PHILLIS LEVIN
May Day
Mercury

PATRICIA LOCKWOOD
Motherland Fatherland
*   Homelandsexuals*

WILLIAM LOGAN
Macbeth in Venice
Madame X
Strange Flesh
The Whispering Gallery

ADRIAN MATEJKA
The Big Smoke
Mixology

MICHAEL MCCLURE
Huge Dreams: San Francisco
*   and Beat Poems*

ROSE MCLARNEY
Its Day Being Gone

DAVID MELTZER
David's Copy: The Selected
*   Poems of David Meltzer*

ROBERT MORGAN
Dark Energy
Terroir

CAROL MUSKE-DUKES
An Octave Above Thunder
Red Trousseau
Twin Cities

ALICE NOTLEY
Culture of One
The Descent of Alette
Disobedience
In the Pines
Mysteries of Small Houses

WILLIE PERDOMO
The Essential Hits of
*   Shorty Bon Bon*

LIA PURPURA
It Shouldn't Have Been
*   Beautiful*

LAWRENCE RAAB
The History of Forgetting
Visible Signs: New and Selected
*   Poems*

BARBARA RAS
The Last Skin
One Hidden Stuff

MICHAEL ROBBINS
Alien vs. Predator
The Second Sex

PATTIANN ROGERS
Generations
Holy Heathen Rhapsody
Wayfare

WILLIAM STOBB
Absentia
Nervous Systems

TRYFON TOLIDES
An Almost Pure Empty Walking

SARAH VAP
Viability

ANNE WALDMAN
Gossamurmur
Kill or Cure
Manatee/Humanity
Structure of the World
*   Compared to a Bubble*

JAMES WELCH
Riding the Earthboy 40

PHILIP WHALEN
Overtime: Selected Poems

ROBERT WRIGLEY
Anatomy of Melancholy and
*   Other Poems*
Beautiful Country
Earthly Meditations: New and
*   Selected Poems*
Lives of the Animals
Reign of Snakes

MARK YAKICH
The Importance of Peeling
*   Potatoes in Ukraine*
Unrelated Individuals Forming
*   a Group Waiting to Cross*